We Carry

by Giulia Verzariu
illustrated by Tom Leonard

Pre-Decodable 14

I0806540

McGraw Hill Education

Bothell, WA • Chicago, IL • Columbus, OH • New York, NY

MHEonline.com

Send all inquiries to:
McGraw-Hill Education
8787 Orion Place
Columbus, OH 43240

ISBN: 978-0-02-145384-9
MHID: 0-02-145384-5

Printed in China

8 9 10 11 12 DSS 28 27 26 25 24

We  a  of .

carry drop water

We  a  of .

carry plate sandwiches

We  a  of .

carry plate grapes

We  a  of .

carry plate apples

We  a  of .

carry bowl salad

See the  of  !

plate

food